THE
COUNTRY DIARY BOOK OF
CREATING A
Butterfly Garden

For my dear
friend Mary —
Do you remember the
day we saw this? —
I miss you —
Love
Hattie
Christmas 1989

Brimstone *Gonopteryx rhamni* female on knapweed
Wingspan 58mm

The Country Diary Book of
CREATING A
Butterfly Garden

E J M Warren

HENRY HOLT AND COMPANY
NEW YORK

To the memory of my parents
B C S & J N Warren

Published in the United States by
Henry Holt and Company, Inc., 115 West 18th Street,
New York, New York 10011.

Originally published in Great Britain by
Webb & Bower (Publishers) Limited
9 Colleton Crescent, Exeter, Devon EX2 4BY.

Library of Congress Catalog Card Number 87–83030

ISBN: 0–8050–0814–4

First American Edition

Design Peter Wrigley

Production Nick Facer/Rob Kendrew

Printed and bound in Italy by Arnoldo Mondadori Editore

10 9 8 7 6 5 4 3 2 1

CONTENTS

Lord, we would serve Thee, and turn to Thy glory,
All our best efforts of mind and of hand;
Lord, we have gardens, and fain would we make Thee,
Master of all their resplendent array.

E G Selwyn

All things bright and beautiful,
    All creatures great and small,
All things wise and wonderful,
    The Lord God made them all.
Each little flower that opens,
    Each little bird that sings,
He made their glowing colours,
    He made their tiny wings.

Mrs C F Alexander

INTRODUCTION

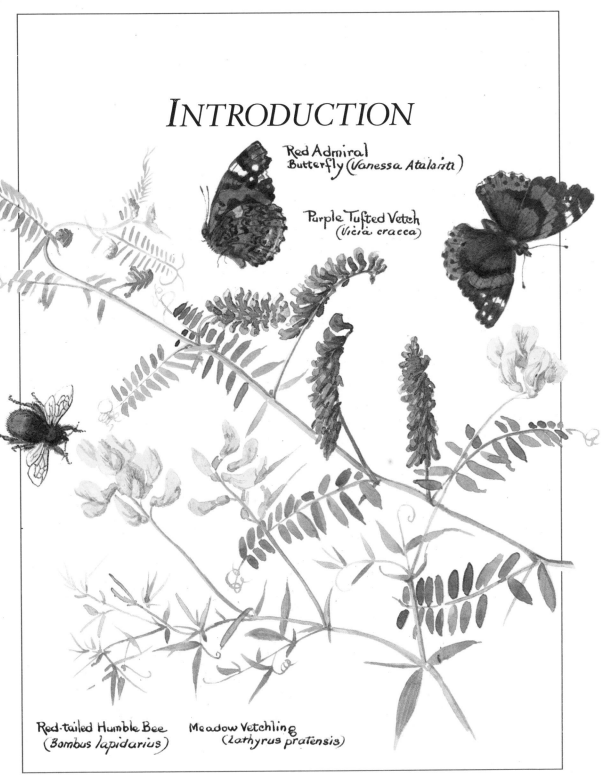

Red Admiral
Butterfly (*Vanessa Atalanta*)

Purple Tufted Vetch
(*Vicia cracca*)

Red-tailed Humble Bee
(*Bombus lapidarius*)

Meadow Vetchling
(*Lathyrus pratensis*)

Few things bring more pleasure to many people than their garden. How much greater the joy if, as well as being filled with beautiful flowers, the garden is alive with butterflies. Alas, today butterflies are becoming increasingly scarce, with many endangered and some actually extinct. The main cause of this increasing scarcity is the destruction of habitat, caused primarily by modern agricultural and forestry methods.

If Edith Holden were alive today and could revisit her favourite haunts I feel sure that she would be horrified by the change in them caused by the destruction of hedgerows and the disappearance of meadows rich in wild flowers and alive with abundant butterflies, which she so enjoyed to watch and recorded so beautifully in her enchanting illustrations.

So great has been the decline in the number of butterflies in the last two decades that people have become alarmed and have begun to wonder how many more species will have become extinct by the year 2000. The Council of Europe has responded by producing a report[1] on threatened European butterflies; special Butterfly Nature Reserves are beginning to be set up to preserve the rarest species; and in Germany the book *Aid Programme for Butterflies*[2]

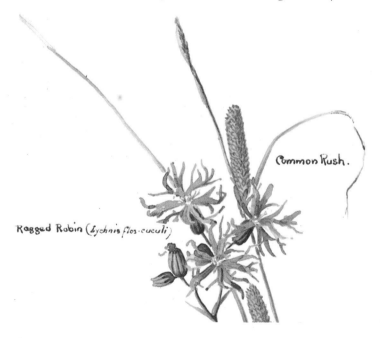

Common Rush.

Ragged Robin (*Lychnis flos-cuculi*)

[1] *Threatened Rhopalocera* (butterflies) *In Europe* by John Heath.
[2] *Hilfsprogramm für Schmetterlinge* by Josef Blab and Otakar Kudrna.

has been published. This outlines an eight-point plan to reverse the decline, by securing adequate areas of habitat for all species outside nature reserves. The eight points are:

— abandonment of intensification of agriculture
— re-establishment of meadows rich in wild flowers
— abandonment of afforestation
— preservation of deciduous woodland and the reintroduction of coppicing
— retention of grassy glades in the middle of woods
— restoration of hedges
— abandonment of the reduction of water tables
— abandonment of the use of insecticides and herbicides

Grizzled Skipper *Pyrgus malvae*
Wingspan 27mm

Painted Lady Butterfly

Without doubt the most important action that can be taken to help butterflies survive is to provide adequate habitat. This is where we all can help by making our gardens into sanctuaries for butterflies and other wildlife. Let no man say his garden is too small, or that it is too large – size does not matter, he can still create a Butterfly Garden. Just pause to think what a wonderful area of good habitat would be created if every garden were converted into a butterfly sanctuary. There is no doubt any garden can help provide much needed habitat for butterflies outside Nature Reserves.

Great Hairy Willow Herb
(Epilobium hirsutum)

By creating a Butterfly Garden I do not mean buying butterflies or chrysalides from a dealer and releasing them in the garden; those who have tried this discover that the released butterflies usually fly straight out again. Rather I hope to show how to attract butterflies naturally present in an area by creating conditions suitable to their needs.

A very bad practice is to buy beautiful looking foreign butterflies

Green Hairstreak *Callophrys rubi* underside
Wingspan 33mm

Wall Butterfly (*Lasiommata Megaera*)

or chrysalides and release them in the garden. They will probably be unable to adapt to our climate and die; but should any such foreign species, or any of its parasites, succeed in establishing itself, it might become a serious pest (as rabbits did when introduced into Australia) due to lack of natural predators. Fortunately this practice is now illegal: under the new Wildlife Act it is an offence to release into the wild any butterfly or moth that is not indigenous to Britain, or a regular, natural immigrant.

Wall Butterfly (Lasiommata Megaera)

Sloe or Blackthorn
(Prunus communis)

Edith Holden drew as she saw things, and occasionally there are anatomical inaccuracies in her beautiful paintings, as in the male Orange Tip, top right page 13.

HOW TO MAKE A BUTTERFLY GARDEN

Orange-tip Butterfly
(Euchloe Cardimines)

Oxe-eye Daisy
(Chrysanthemum leucanthemum)

Purple Clover
(Trifolium pratense)

White or Dutch Clover
(Trifolium repens)

Meadow Fox-Tail Grass
(Alopecurus pratensis)

Plants and shrubs for butterflies fall into two categories: nectar plants for adult butterflies and food plants for caterpillars (larval food plant) and there are both garden and wild plants in each category. The way to create a Butterfly Garden is to grow both sorts for the butterfly species which are found in your area, and so to attract them to dwell in your garden. To find out which butterflies do occur in your area, try to obtain a local list. Such local lists are often produced by Natural History societies and may be obtained from them, or from the local Public Library (also see pp 138–139).

NEVER use any herbicides (weedkillers), insecticides, fungicides, slug, snail, worm or mole killers, or lawndressings (which usually contain weed and worm killers), or any other chemicals. They are quite unnecessary and their results can look repulsive: brown patches of dead and dying plants in a desert-like waste. Do not destroy. Do not further contaminate the environment. Instead,

Large Garden White Butterfly
(Pieris Brassicae)

Herb Robert
(Geranium Robertianum)

Godetias

Wood Anemone or Wind-flower
(Anemone membrosa.)

English Stonecrop *Sedum anglicum* and Thyme *Thymus serpyllum*

Daisy
(*Bellis perennis*)

Red Admiral *Vanessa atalanta* on *Sedum spectabile*
Wingspan 67mm

build your plants up by feeding them well and regularly with harmless seaweed manure (Maxicrop or Sea Bounty), and sequestered iron. Top dress with Acta Bacta, Forest Bark, peat and sterilized bone-meal. Never use unsterilized bone-meal; it is highly dangerous, because it is possible to catch diseases such as anthrax from it. Well fed plants are much less likely to fall victims of diseases or pests. Be prepared to share your garden with all forms of wildlife great and small, birds and animals, insects and plants. If you do so, they will provide you with an abiding and absorbing new interest.

Small Copper *Lycaena phlaeas*
Wingspan 32mm

Wall Butterfly

Small Garden White

Meadow Buttercup
(Ranunculous acris)
Common Bugle (Ajuga reptans)
Yellow Heartsease (Viola tricolor)

Large Flowered Bitter Cress
(Cardamine amara)
Yellow Weasel Snout (Galeobdolen luteum)

Pasture Lousewort (*Pedicularis sylvatica*)

On large sheets of graph paper make a scale plan of your garden and its contents and study it to see where you can add plants and shrubs suited to your local butterflies. Rather than pull up established plants and shrubs think of adding more and different varieties. Before getting rid of weeds, check how many might be essential caterpillar food plants, for although you may attract butterflies to your garden by providing attractive nectar plants, they will not breed there unless their larval food plants are also present. Before starting work in the garden, try to mark all your intended additions and alterations on the plan, so that you can visualize the garden as a whole.

The first most useful piece of equipment that you can get is a small GREENHOUSE, which will enable you to grow annual and perennial garden and wild flowers from SEED. Growing from seed will provide both a far greater number of plants than you could afford to buy, and a far wider range of interesting varieties than you could obtain ready grown. The second most useful piece of garden equipment is a HOSE. This is invaluable, for watering is the most important piece of care which can be given to a garden. The hose should be stored on a reel fixed to the wall of the house close to an outside tap, always ready for use.

Always try to plant in MASSES – preferably of one colour rather than mixed – NOT in single plants. Masses are both more effective – producing a strikingly beautiful garden which people will stop

OPPOSITE ABOVE: Pearl-bordered Fritillary *Boloria euphrosyne*
Wingspan 44mm

OPPOSITE BELOW: Small Pearl-bordered Fritillary *Boloria selene*
Wingspan 41mm

White Stonecrop *Sedum album*

Fox-glove (*Digitalis purpurea*)
Trailing Rose (*Rosa arvensis*)

to admire – and much more likely to catch the attention of passing butterflies and draw them into the garden. Buy shrubs as these take several years to grow from seed or cuttings; but you can then increase your stock by growing seeds or cuttings taken from your own shrubs.

Try to leave part of your garden completely wild, with a patch of hay and all kinds of wild flowers. It is possible to buy packets of mixed wild flower seeds to create such a wild flower hay meadow for butterflies, from Dobies, Thompson & Morgan, or John Chambers. The hay patch should be cut with sickles or scythes only once a year, in early September. Also try leaving a patch of grass, possibly a bank, completely rough and never cutting it at all; this might be used by some of the Browns and Skippers to breed. When choosing garden flowers try to avoid double flowers. Single flowers with large centres from which to obtain nectar are much more favoured by the butterflies. Roses are no good at all for butterflies; have some for yourself by all means, but provide plenty of other plants for butterflies.

Don't be too worried about weeds. Some people spend all their time pulling out weeds or soaking the garden with weedkillers.

Fine-leaved Heath.
(Erica cinerea)

Cross-leaved Heath
(Erica Tetralix)

Silver-studded Blue *Plebejus argus* male
Wingspan 31mm

Heather or Ling
(*Calluna vulgaris*)

Daffodils

Such people usually have the ugliest gardens because they are destructive, not constructive. Spend your time putting things into your garden, not taking them out. Put in plenty of flowers and shrubs, and plant them a little closer together than the garden books advise, then there will be less space left for weeds to utilize. I never use any poisonous chemicals whatsoever, yet people always stop to admire my garden.

Do not worry about weeding shrubberies. Let the grass and wild flowers grow naturally between the shrubs, and just cut once a year in autumn. Alternatively, plant ground cover plants such as *Ajuga pyramidalis*, *A reptans*, *Bergenia* species, *Campanula garganica*, *C portenschlagiana*, *C poscharskyana*, *Geranium endressii*, *G sanguineum*, *Hypericum calycinum*, *H × moserianum*,

Daffodils
(Narcissus pseudo-narcissus)

Lamium species, *Polygonatum* × *hybridum*, *Pulmonaria officinalis*, *Vinca major*, *V minor* between the shrubs and let them spread until they cover the whole of the ground and naturally exclude the weeds. Keep a small piece of lawn nicely mown near the house. Turn the rest of the grass into a hay meadow. Nothing is more annoying and tiring than large areas of lawn which are always having to be mown.

Common Eye-bright
(*Euphrasia officinalis*)

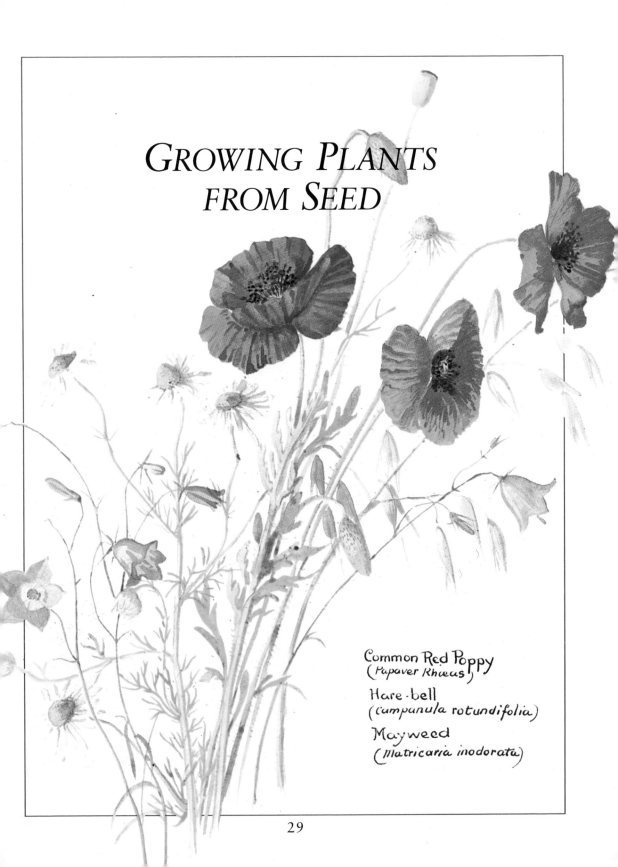

GROWING PLANTS FROM SEED

Common Red Poppy
(Papaver Rhœas)

Hare-bell
(Campanula rotundifolia)

Mayweed
(Matricaria inodorata)

Some annual flowers can be grown by sowing the seed directly into the soil where the plants are to flower. The soil has first to be broken up to a fine tilth. Such outdoor sowings have to be watered very carefully every day or the little seedlings will die off. When they are three or four weeks old the young seedlings will need to be thinned out to the required flowering distance.

Most flowers however can be much more successfully grown by planting the seeds in early spring in plastic seed trays filled with John Innes or some other proprietary seed compost, in a greenhouse or, if you have not got one, indoors. For speedy germination place the trays in the airing cupboard until the seeds sprout (about four days to a week), then put them in a sunny window – though they may need to be shaded in very sunny weather.

After about three weeks prick the seedlings out carefully into

Tobacco plant Sensation mixed

larger trays, or pots, filled with John Innes No 1 potting compost. When they have settled down and started to grow larger gradually harden them off by either opening the greenhouse windows, or putting the trays or pots out on the patio for lengthening periods of time during the day. When fully hardened off – about three weeks – the small plants can be planted out in the garden. Always soak the seed trays well with water, preferably with Maxicrop or Phostrogen added, an hour before starting to plant out the seedlings.

SLUGS AND SNAILS

If slugs and snails become a problem with young seedlings, collect them carefully in a box and take them out in the country and set them free in a damp hedgerow or wooded verge.

BEES

Bees are among the best helpers any gardener can have because they pollinate the flowers and thereby increase the fruitfulness. Any garden buzzing with bees is likely to be much more flourishing than one without them. Fortunately most plants which are attrac-

Flower of Lime
or Linden Tree
(Tilia Europæa)

Common Bumble Bee
(Bombus terrestris)

Hive Bee
(Apis mellifica)

Orange Tip *Anthocharis cardamines*
Wingspan 46mm

Germander Speedwell
(*Veronica chamædris*)

Large Skipper *Ochlodes venatus*
Wingspan 33mm

Pasque Flower
(anemone pulsatella)

33

tive to butterflies are also attractive to bees. If you like you can have a special Bee Border in your garden: first plant a row of borage at the back, then *Limnanthes douglasii* over the rest of the border, with alternating lavender bushes and clumps of Six Hills catmint among the *Limnanthes douglasii*. Such a border will not only be a magnet for all the bees for miles around, but will also attract many butterflies.

BIRDS

It has been said that if one wants butterflies in one's garden one should not encourage birds, but I have found that they manage to coexist in my garden. I feed the birds from mid October to April on canary seed, mixed millet, sunflower seeds, dried fruit, meat

Marbled White *Melanargia galathea* on thistle
Wingspan 58mm

Goldfinch
feeding on
Thistle-seed

fat, cheese, peanuts and ripe pears. DO NOT give desiccated coconut, raw rice, or white bread: these are all bad for birds and can cause digestive troubles. DO NOT give peanuts after 23 March, as they are fatal to baby tits. I give water all the year round.

It is true that many birds feed their young on caterpillars, but they also feed them on enormous quantities of greenfly and all kinds of other grubs. You can always protect caterpillars in your garden by sleeving them (see p 51) or by rearing them in cages. Unless you happen to have a shrike, I think you will be able to enjoy both butterflies and birds in your garden.

HOW TO MAKE THE MOST OF YOUR BUTTERFLY GARDEN

Red Campion
(Lychnis diurna)
Wild Hyacinth
(agraphis nutans)
Wild Beaked Parsley
(anthriscus sylvestris)

With everything one does, the more one puts into it, the more one gets out of it. This is as true of Butterfly Gardens as of anything else. Three ways to increase your pleasure in a Butterfly Garden are: keeping a diary, making a photographic record, and rearing caterpillars.

DIARY

A daily written record or diary of your garden, the weather and the butterflies seen could be of great interest. It can be kept in an excercise book, a diary – or even a five-year diary, which would enable you to compare entries with those for the same day in preceding years. Or your diary could be kept on a 'year at a view' office planner on the wall, where you could see the whole year at

Cowslip (*Primula veris*)

White Admiral *Limenitis camilla* ABOVE: upperside
BELOW: underside Wingspan 64mm

one time. In fact you could make your own Garden Diary just as Edith Holden made her Country Diary; and if you can draw or paint, try to illustrate it like she did.

Try to record the weather each day as concisely as possible, perhaps with letters, for example: S for sunny, C for Cloudy, R for rain, TH for thunder, SN for snow, and so on. Give the wind direction – N, E, S, or W – and give the highest temperature for each day, for example 60°F (15°C). Record when the first flower opens on each kind of plant, and when the first leaves appear in the spring. Typical entries might read:

> '14 January, 1st snowdrop out'; '4 March, 1st daffodil out'; '23 March, sticky buds opening on horse chestnut tree'.

Either in the same book or chart, or a separate one, record all the species of butterfly seen in your garden each season. Note the dates of the first sightings of each species. Note *all* the species seen each day. Note the abundance of each species during the season, eg single specimen, scarce, common, abundant, or mass. Note which nectar flowers are most visited and by which species. Make a special note of which coloured flowers attract which species. If you see a butterfly laying eggs, note what plant it is laying on. Note what resting places are chosen for the night. Use field glasses to watch any butterflies that you cannot get close to without disturbing, just as one does for bird-watching. Try to determine whether butterflies are male or female by looking at their markings.

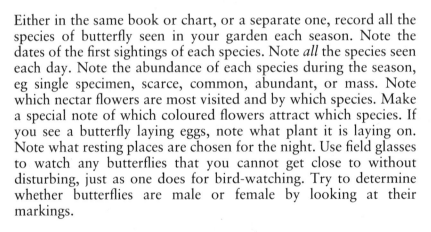

Peacock Butterfly and Larva.

Peacock *Inachis io*
Wingspan 63mm

PHOTOGRAPHY

Try to photograph all the butterflies and caterpillars and flowers and shrubs throughout the year in your Butterfly Garden, preferably in colour. Whatever kind of camera you possess, have a go and see what you can do. A skilful photographer can achieve remarkably good results with quite simple apparatus.

To achieve the finest results you need a light weight 35mm single lens reflex (SLR) camera with adjustable focussing, used with a 105mm or 100mm macro lens. The latter will focus from infinity down to about half life size and with the addition of an auto extension ring will take life size photographs of butterflies.

Automatic cameras can be used but should preferably have manual override. The focussing screen should be plain, fine grain type, no fresnel lens, no split image. An auto-wind or a motor drive are excellent, worth every penny and best used in S setting.

Orange Tip *Anthocharis cardamines* underside Wingspan 46mm

Silver-studded Blue *Plebejus argus*: male (RIGHT) and female (LEFT)
Wingspan 31mm

Gatekeeper *Pyronia tithonus*
Wingspan 40mm

Comma *Polygonia c-album*
Wingspan 55mm

Macro-zoom lenses, 2× macro converters and bellows units are generally best avoided.

Also excellent are the 2¼″ × 2¼″ twin lens reflex cameras, which, when used with additional close up lenses and parallax corrector will focus down to 12″. These cameras, though heavier, have the advantage of giving the larger format transparencies which are good for reproduction and projection.

Always use good quality films. Never use cheap films, they will spoil your best efforts. Try to use natural light rather than flash, it will give much more natural results. Always use a lens hood. Good films for transparencies are Agfachrome 50 RS Professional, CT 100 and CT 200, High Speed Ektachrome, Kodachrome 25 and 64, and Fujichrome 400. For colour prints use Agfacolor XR 100, XR 200 or XR 400. Slow speed, fine grain films such as

Speckled Wood *Pararge aegeria* underside
Wingspan 47mm

Agfachrome 50 RS Professional or Kodachrome 25 will give much the best quality transparencies, though they may entail using a tripod to avoid camera shake. In my opinion Agfachrome gives the best colours.

If you wish to try to photograph butterflies in flight you will need a camera with a fast shutter speed of at least 1/000 sec.

To photograph butterflies set the shutter speed and aperture and focus down to the shortest distance possible, then walk slowly and quietly towards the butterfly, taking the picture when the butterfly comes into focus in the viewfinder. If you have any cater-

Essex Skipper *Thymelicus lineolus*
Wingspan 27mm

pillars in your garden, try photographing them too – also any eggs or chrysalides you can find. You might even be lucky enough to be able to take a series of photographs of a butterfly emerging from its chrysalis.

For butterflies which are moving their wings or are liable to fly off, use a fast shutter speed such as 1/500 at f/5.6 or 1/1000 at f/4 in bright light (film speed ASA 50). But where the butterfly is sitting still and unlikely to move (eg a Blue with wings closed on a flower-head) use a small stop such as f/22 and 1/25 or f/16 and 1/50 (film speed ASA 50). The much smaller stop will increase the depth of field and improve the focus of the whole picture, providing that you can hold the camera steady at the slower speeds.

If you want to use an exposure meter, TTL (through the lens) metering is the best for butterfly photography. But very good photographs can be taken without any exposure meter at all: simply learn the stop and shutter speed combinations for good light given in the film maker's instruction leaflet off by heart and stick to them. For films with a speed of ASA 50 these would be f/22 and 1/25 or f/5.6 and 1/500. For photographs taken in the shade increase the exposure 3×, eg f/8 and 1/25. In normal lighting conditions photographs exposed by this method will be very successful, but there may be some failures in poor lighting conditions.

To get photographs of blue butterflies or flowers to come out a good blue colour, try to take them in the shade on a bright day at 3× the exposure you would use in the sun, (eg f/8 and 1/25 on ASA 50); or on a lightly overcast day at 2× the normal exposure (eg f/11 and 1/25 on ASA 50). Sunlight spoils blue colours and makes them tend to come out purple in colour photographs.

Orange-tip Butterfly
(Euchloe Cardimines)

Purple Clover
(Trifolium pratense)

When trying to photograph butterflies or to observe them closely, wear dull, medium coloured clothing, neither black nor white nor fluorescent nor pastel colours. Best are tweeds, flannel, linen or corduroy, with woollen knitwear and non-shiny anoraks in leaf green, grey, bracken brown, slate blue or dull brick red. Good photography requires much patience, perseverance and practice.

Silver-studded Blue *Plebejus argus* male
Wingspan 31mm

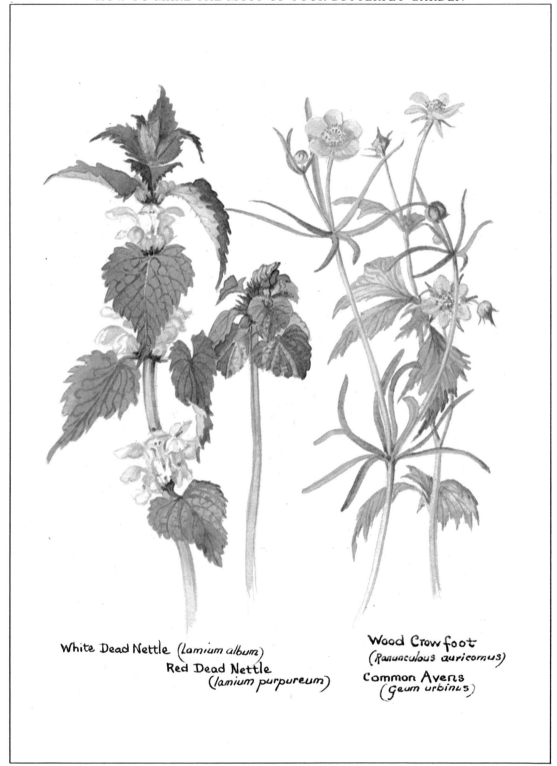

White Dead Nettle *(Lamium album)*
Red Dead Nettle
(Lamium purpureum)

Wood Crowfoot
(Ranunculous auricomus)
Common Avens
(Geum urbinus)

REARING CATERPILLARS

If you are lucky enough to see a butterfly laying eggs or to find caterpillars in your garden, you can try to rear them, either by 'sleeving' or in breeding cages.

For the beginner it is easier to sleeve. Wrap green nylon netting loosely round the area of the food plant where the caterpillars are feeding, leaving it growing in the ground, and tie the netting tightly at both ends, placing a small piece of plastic foam round the stem under the tie, so that it resembles a Christmas cracker. Caterpillars are Houdinis! It must be tied tightly or they will be out! This protects the caterpillars from birds, and prevents them from wandering away. If all the food plant inside the sleeve is getting eaten, transfer them to a fresh part of the same plant. As they grow you will have to enclose larger areas — and ensure that you have enclosed sufficient stems for them to chrysalis on.

Alternatively you can put the caterpillars in a caterpillar cage, either in a cool but light room in the house, or in a greenhouse, or in a sheltered place in the garden. Be very careful to feed the caterpillars on the plant on which you found them, for all caterpillars will only eat their own food plants and if fed on the wrong plant will probably die. Food should always be fresh and dry. The food plant can either be picked and placed in a small glass vase of water — being careful always to stop up the neck of the vase with cotton wool so that the caterpillars cannot get into the water and drown — or a plant can be dug up and planted in a small — preferably clay — flowerpot. Circular plastic cages sold for rearing caterpillars are bad, because the caterpillars cannot grip the shiny surface to climb up and down the sides. It is much better to make

ABOVE LEFT: Red Admiral *Vanessa atalanta* emerging from chrysalis
ABOVE: Newly emerged Red Admiral and empty chrysalis
BELOW LEFT: Red Admiral growing its wings beside empty chrysalis

your own cages, either in wooden boxes or of nylon netting over a wire frame. Simplest is to get an old lampshade frame, with the shade material removed, and place it upside down on top of a flowerpot containing a growing food plant, and cover it with green nylon netting, tying the netting tightly with string (not a rubber band) round the sides of the flowerpot.

Large White caterpillars on turnip inside caterpillar
cage constructed from lampshade frame

Best is to get a sound wooden box with a rough inside surface, approximately two feet by one foot by one foot — but it could be larger or smaller according to the size of food plant you want to put in it. Stand the box on end, so that the top will form the cage front. If the box had a lid this could be used either to make a division down the middle to make two compartments, or to make a raised floor. A raised floor requires a small circular hole cut in the middle, and is fixed so as to leave room for a small glass vase

Inside caterpillar cage made from wooden box are Comma caterpillars
on currant (LEFT) and Red Admiral caterpillars on stinging nettle (RIGHT)

of water – an empty cosmetic jar or similar will do – to stand in
the cage underneath the raised floor. Push the stems of the appropriate
cut food plant through the hole into the water and pack the
hole with cotton wool. Cut large windows in the sides of the cage,
and cover them with perforated zinc or nylon netting to allow air
into the cage. The zinc or netting should be tightly fixed in place
by screwing small pieces of wooden beading over it round the
edges of the opening.

The front of the cage is enclosed by a sheet of glass, which slides
up and down in grooves between two pieces of beading. This lifts
right out for cleaning and filling the cage and when in place allows

the occupants to be conveniently observed. Care must be taken to see that everything fits tightly because caterpillars can escape through amazingly small spaces. Cover the floor with a sheet of blotting paper or paper kitchen towel which should be removed each time the food is changed and a clean piece inserted.

Greater Bird's-foot Trefoil
(*lotus major*)

Caterpillars can be moved from stale to fresh food with a small paint-brush, or by standing a stem of the old food to which they are attached in among the fresh food. Some moth caterpillars need a small tray of earth on the floor of the cage in which to bury when they are ready to chrysalis. Caterpillars like the rough inside of a wooden cage, and climb the walls as they would the trunk of a tree, often hanging up on them to split or to chrysalis.

Very small caterpillars can be reared in small circular caterpillar tins with glass lids. Line the floor of the tin with blotting paper, and put in one or two leaves of food plant without any water; fresh leaves must be given every day. Some caterpillars are cannibals — especially those of the Orange Tip — and must be reared singly.

Simple additional cages for an emergency can be made from cardboard shoe boxes. Stand the box on end, place the caterpillars

Meadow Brown *Maniola jurtina*
Wingspan 50mm

Meadow Brown *Maniola jurtina* underside
Wingspan 50mm

Cardboard shoe box cage for caterpillars with Speckled Wood
caterpillars on couch grass

and their food plant in a pot or vase inside, and cover the front
with green nylon netting fastened by tying string round and round
the sides of the box over the netting.

The duration of the larval and pupal stages varies from species
to species, being sometimes only a few weeks, sometimes many
months. If you have overwintering chrysalides in the house, keep
the cage in an unheated room, otherwise they will emerge too
early. When you think your chrysalides are due to emerge, be sure
there are some bushy twigs in the cage for the butterflies to hold
on to while their wings grow. Also a few nice nectar flowers –

ABOVE: Knapweed *Centaurea scabiosa*

LEFT: Peacock caterpillar on nettle

such as knapweed or buddleia – should be put in the food plant vase, so that the butterflies may have a feed if they wish before you release them. If no nectar flowers are available, a bottle feed can be made for them by mixing a scant teaspoonful of honey and a scant teaspoonful of caster sugar together in a cupful of warm water. Put a little of this mixture in a small dish – a lens out of an old pair of spectacles is good – on the floor of the cage for the butterflies to drink from. When the wings are fully grown – after about three or four hours – release the butterflies in the garden.

CHOOSING THE RIGHT FLOWERS

Meadow
Crane's-bill
(Geranium pratense)

Yellow Toadflax
(Linaria vulgaris)

Common Ragwort
(Senicis jacobéa)

Butterflies are attracted to flowers by their nectar, their scent, and their colour: those with the most nectar and the sweetest scent attracting the most butterflies.

Purple and yellow appear to be the most popular flower colours with butterflies eg buddleias, lavender, thistles, knapweed, scabious, asters, and bird's foot trefoil, dandelions and most similar looking flowers. They also like pink and reddish mauve but do not appear to favour scarlet. They also appear to prefer light and medium shades to dark shades.

Butterflies also try to choose flowers and plants which match their own colours to roost in. For instance Clouded Yellows choose yellow flowers or leaves which are turning yellow, Whites choose white flowers or the white undersides of leaves, and the Brimstone chooses the pale green underside of leaves.[1]

[1] J A Simes, *Entomologist* **75**:247

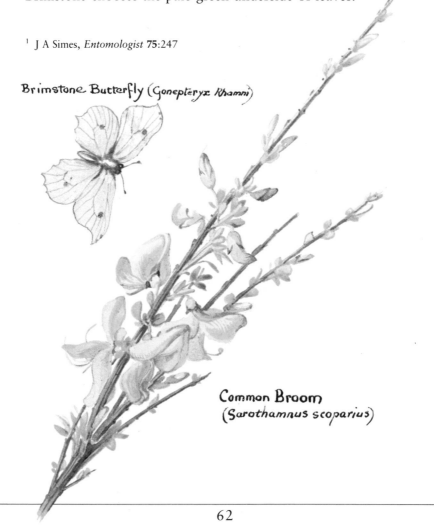

Brimstone Butterfly (*Gonepteryx Rhamni*)

Common Broom
(*Sarothamnus scoparius*)

Cuckoo flower *Cardamine pratensis*

BUDDLEIAS

Without doubt the most important garden plant for butterflies is that well known shrub, buddleia. If you have one buddleia in your garden you are almost certain to have some butterflies, but if you have a large number of buddleias you will attract all the butterflies in the neighbourhood. So keen are butterflies on buddleia, that if they are present the butterflies will ignore all other good butterfly flowers and congregate on the buddleias.

If you have a small garden try to have at least one or two buddleias; but if you have a medium or large garden, why not have a buddleia hedge? Plant a row of buddleia bushes leaving about four feet between each and let them gradually grow into one another, pruning hard each spring in late March. Or the

Clouded Yellow *Colias crocea* underside
Wingspan 57mm

branches can be tied down to a fence, stakes, or Netlon on a wall, and interwoven into one another when young in the same way as climbing roses, and then pruned back to this original framework each spring.

There are several different kinds of buddleia and all are attractive to butterflies, so it is worth having some of each. Some are not as hardy as *Buddleia davidii* and need warm sheltered positions. *Buddleia davidii* will grow anywhere provided the soil does not get waterlogged. Butterflies like the pale coloured buddleias such as the original pale mauve *Buddleia davidii* or the pink coloured Fascination better than the darker shades such as Royal Red. Buddleias can be grown easily from seed or cuttings to increase your stock, though those grown from seed may not be true to the colour of the parent bush.

The following is a list of different kinds of buddleia, all well worth growing.

BUDDLEIA DAVIDII VARIETIES

Buddleia davidii	lilac
Black Knight	dark blue purple
Charming	pink
Empire Blue	violet blue with orange eye
Fascination	pink (a special favourite with butterflies)
Fortune	lilac with an orange eye
Ile de France	intense bright purple
Magnifica	bluish purple
Peace	white
Royal Red	striking rich reddish purple
Veitchiana	deep lavender purple
White Bouquet	white with yellow centre
White Profusion	white

OTHER SPECIES OF BUDDLEIA

Buddleia alternifolia	very sweet scented lavender blue flowers on old wood. June.
Buddleia colvilei	rose red flowers on old wood. June. Best grown in a sunny sheltered spot against a wall. Averse to pruning.
Buddleia crispa (synonym *B. paniculata*)	fragrant lilac-pink flowers with orange eye on current year's shoots. July.
Buddleia fallowiana Lochinch	fragrant lavender blue flowers on current year's shoots. July to September.

Buddleia globosa	orange ball-shaped flowers in May. Prune after flowering.
Buddleia nanhoensis	a dwarf bush of elegant habit.
Buddleia weyeriana hybrid	orange yellow ball-shaped flowers in summer.

STINGING NETTLES

One of the most important wild plants for butterflies is the common stinging nettle *Urtica dioica*. Nettles are the larval food plant of most of the Vanessid butterflies. But it is not sufficient just to grow stinging nettles, they must be carefully managed and sited. Butterflies are very fussy about their nettles, they do not like

Small Tortoiseshell
(*Vanessa Urticæ*)

Stinging Nettle
(*Urtica Dioica*)

them tough. Females will only lay where the nettles are growing in a sheltered sunny situation, if possible in a hollow and facing south, where there will be tender young shoots coming on for the caterpillars when they hatch.

To obtain nettles pull up some plants with runners from the edge of a wild nettle patch. In the wild nettles are often found growing against the side of a cow shed, so try some against the most sunny sheltered side of your tool shed. Look if there is a hollow anywhere in your garden, and if there is, plant some nettles there. I have had great success with a small patch of nettles growing on the bank sloping down to the basement windows of my house. If there is no suitable hollow in your garden, dig out a hole like a golf course bunker, approximately six feet long by three feet wide by two feet deep. Throw all the earth out to the north side as you dig, thus forming a bank to shelter the bunker. Make the bottom slope down gradually from ground level at one side to three feet deep at the bank side. Plant a blackthorn hedge on top of the bank to give even more shelter. Plant nettles in the bunker.

Red Admiral
Butterfly (*Vanessa Atalanta*)

Cut down one third of the nettle patch in early June, one third in July, and one third in August, thus ensuring a continuing supply of young shoots for the females to lay on. Cut down the whole bed again in December. Be very careful when you are doing the cutting that you do not throw out any eggs, caterpillars, or chrysalides. Eggs are often on the under surface of the leaves (Small Tortoiseshell, Peacock) but may also be on the upperside (Red Admiral, Comma), caterpillars may be in batches or single, in webs or concealed in rolled up leaves (Red Admiral).

GORSE

Although Gorse (*Ulex europaeus*) is a good butterfly plant don't grow it anywhere near a house, or in large breaks anywhere, because in dry weather it becomes tinder dry and creates a serious fire risk.

In the following list of other good nectar plants for adult butterflies those which are also larval food plants are marked F.

RECOMMENDED FOR THE BUTTERFLY GARDEN

SHRUBS AND TREES

	Caryopteris clandonensis	
	Ceanothus species	especially *C dentatus*
	Choisya ternata	
	Cistus species	rock rose
	Colletia armata	a very fragrant Chilean shrub
F	*Colutea arborescens*	bladder senna
F	*Cornus sanguinea*	dogwood
F	*Crataegus monogyna*	hawthorn

May or Hawthorn
(*Crataegus oxycantha*)

F	*Cytisus* species	broom
F	*Erica* and	
	Calluna species	heaths and heathers

Fruit of
Wild Cornel or Dogwood (Cornus sanguinea)

Privet (Ligustrum vulgare)

F	*Frangula alnus*	alder buckthorn
	Hebes	
	(formerly veronica)	especially *H* Great Orme, *H salcifolia* and *H speciosa* varieties
	Helianthemum species	rock rose
	Juniperus communis	juniper
	Lavandula species	lavender
	Ligustrum species	privet
F	*Lonicera* species	honeysuckle
F	*Prunus spinosa*	blackthorn
F	*Rhamnus catharticus*	buckthorn
	Ribes sanguineum	flowering currant
	Rosmarinus	rosemary
F	*Rubus* species	all flowering species, especially *R fruticosus* bramble, which is a great favourite with many species of butterfly
	Senecio laxifolius	
	Spiraea bumalda	
	Anthony Waterer	
	Syringa species	lilac, especially mauve and purple single flowered
	Tamarix gallica	tamarisk
	Viburnams	single flowered species, but not *V opulus* Sterile the Snowball Tree, which is useless
F	*Betula pendula*	silver birch (attractive to the Speckled Wood)

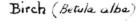

Birch (*Betula alba*)

Blackthorn *Prunus spinosa*

Catkins of Aspen (Populus trémula)
Purple Willow (Salix purpures) Goat Willow or Round-leaved Sallow
and   (Salix caprea)
Alder (Alnus glutinosa)

F	*Corylus avellana*	hazel
F	*Hedera helix*	ivy
F	*Ilex aquifolium*	holly
F	*Populus* species	poplars
F	*Prunus* species	cherries
F	*Salix* species	willows
	Sambucus species	elder
F	*Sorbus* species	rowans
F	*Ulmus* species	elms

GARDEN FLOWERS

	Ageratum houstonianum	ageratum
	Alyssum saxatile	gold dust
	Antirrhinum	snapdragon
	Arabis albida	rock cress, pink and white
	Armeria species	thrift, sea pink
	Aster novi-belgii	Michaelmas daisies, especially pink or pale mauve single varieties
	Aubrieta deltoidea	aubretia
F	*Borago officinalis*	borage
	Campanula species	
	Centaurea cyanus	cornflower
	Centaurea dealbata C *macrocephala*	knapweeds
	Centranthus ruber	valerian. Pink is better than red or white
	Cheiranthus species	wallflowers, especially purple and yellow
	Chrysanthemums	single annual species and ox-eye daisies
	Coreopsis species	
	Cosmos species	
	Delphinium species	delphiniums, especially pale blue varieties
F	*Dianthus barbatus*	sweet williams
	Echium plantagineum	dwarf hybrids
	Erigeron species	
	Eryngium maritimum	sea holly
	Godetias	dwarf mixed
	Helenium autumnale	
	Helianthus	sunflowers
	Heliotropium	heliotrope
F	*Hesperis matronalis*	sweet rocket, dames violet, mauve or white, very good nectar and food plant
	Hyssopus	hyssop
	Iberis species	candytuft
	Kniphofia species	red-hot pokers
	Lathyrus latifolius	everlasting pea; good for Brimstones
	Layia elegans	

ABOVE: Lavender and sweet williams

RIGHT: Green-veined White *Pieris napi*
Wingspan 50mm
roosting for the night on delphiniums

Large Garden White Butterfly
(*Pieris Brassicae*)

	Lobularia maritima	alyssum, white and purple Royal Carpet
	Limnanthes douglasii	poached egg flower
F	*Lunaria* species	honesty
	Matthiola species	stocks
	Nepeta × faassenii	catmint, especially Six Hills Giant
	Nicotiana affinis	tobacco plant, especially Sensation Mixed
	Oenothera species	evening primrose
	Pelargoniums	
	Petunias	especially single varieties for butterflies, but for yourself Double Circus is outstanding
	Phlox species	all kinds from four foot herbaceous border species to the dwarf *Phlox drummondii* Twinkling Stars
F	*Primulas*	primulas, primrose and polyanthus

Primrose
(Primula vulgaris)

F	*Reseda odorata*	mignonette; make seed bed very firm
F	*Scabiosa* species	especially pale shades of the annual varieties
	Sedum spectabile	ice plant, the pale pink varieties, not Autumn Joy
	Solidago canadensis	golden rod
	Tagetes patula	dwarf French marigolds especially single Marietta varieties and double Spanish Brocade
F	*Tropaeolum majus*	nasturtiums
	Verbena	

Silver-spotted Skipper *Hesperia comma* underside
Wingspan 31mm

WILD FLOWERS

	Ajuga reptans	bugle
F	*Alliaria petiolata*	garlic mustard, Jack by the hedge
	Anthriscus sylvestris	cow parsley
F	*Anthyllis vulneraria*	kidney vetch
	Armeria maritima	thrift, sea pink
	Bellis perennis	daisy
F	*Carduus, Carlina* and	
	Cirsium species	thistles – most attractive
	Centaurea cyanus	cornflower
	Centaurea nigra	knapweed – one of the most attractive of all flowers to many species of butterfly
	Clematis vitalba	old man's beard, traveller's joy
F	*Coronilla varia*	crown vetch
F	*Daucus carota*	wild carrot
	Dianthus species	pinks
	Dipsacus fullonium	teasel
F	*Echium vulgare*	viper's bugloss
	Endymion nonscriptus	bluebell
	Epilobium angustifolium	rose-bay willowherb
	Erodium cicutarium	common stork's bill
	Eupatorium cannabinum	hemp agrimony
	Filipendula ulmaria	meadowsweet
F	*Foeniculum vulgare*	fennel
F	*Fragaria vesca*	wild strawberry
	Galium verum	lady's bedstraw
F	*Helianthemum nummularium*	common rock rose
	Hieracium species	hawkweeds
F	*Hippocrepis comosa*	horseshoe vetch
F	*Knautia arvensis*	scabious
	Lamium purpureum	red dead-nettle
F	*Lathyrus* species	vetchlings
	Leucanthemum vulgare	ox-eye daisy
	Lilium martagon	martagon lily
	Limonium species	sea-lavender

Meadow Sweet
or
Queen of the Meadow
(*Spiræa salicifolia*)

ABOVE: Nodding thistle *Carduus mutans*
BELOW: Common mallow *Malva sylvestris*

ABOVE: Red campion *Silene dioica*
OPPOSITE ABOVE: Narrow-leaved vetch *Vicia angustifolia*
OPPOSITE BELOW: Thrift, or sea pink, *Armeria maritima*

F	*Lotus corniculatus*	bird's foot trefoil – a very important nectar plant and larval food plant
	Malva sylvestris	mallow
F	*Medicago sativa*	lucerne, alfalfa
F	*Melampyrum pratense*	cow wheat
	Mentha aquatica	water mint – most attractive to butterflies
	Onobrychis viciifolia	sainfoin
F	*Ononis* species	rest-harrows
F	*Origanum vulgare*	marjoram
F	*Peucedanum palustre*	milk parsley
	Plantago species	plantains
	Potentilla species	cinquefoils
F	*Primula veris*	cowslip
F	*Primula vulgaris*	primrose
	Pulsatilla vulgaris	pasque flower
	Ranunculus acris	buttercup
F	*Reseda lutea*	wild mignonette
	Rosa canina	dog rose
	Rosa rubiginosa	sweet briar

Dog Roses (*Rosa canina*)
Honey suckle (*Lonicera caprifolium*)

F	*Rubus fruticosus*	bramble – a great favourite with many species
F	*Rumex* species	docks and sorrels
	Sanguisorba officinalis	great burnet
	Sedum species	stonecrops, especially *S album*
	Senecio jacobaea	ragwort
	Silene vulgaris, *S dioica, S acaulis*	bladder, red and moss campions
F	*Sinapis arvensis*	charlock
	Succisa pratensis	devil's bit scabious
	Taraxacum section *Vulgaria*	dandelions – and other similar looking yellow flowers

Small Skipper *Thymelicus flavus*: male (BELOW) and female (ABOVE)
Wingspan 30mm

Painted Lady Butterfly
(Vanessa atalanta)

Bilberry or Whortleberry
(Vacoinium myrtilis)

	Thymus serpyllum	thyme
F	*Trifolium* species	clovers
	Vaccinium myrtillus	bilberry
F	*Vicia* species	vetches
	Vinca species	periwinkles
F	*Viola canina,*	
	V *odorata*	dog violet, sweet violet

GRASSES

F	*Agropyron repens*	couch
F	*Aira praecox*	early hair
F	*Brachypodium*	
	sylvaticum	false brome
F	*Bromus* species	brome
F	*Dactylis glomerata*	cocksfoot
F	*Deschampsia*	
	caespitosa	tufted hair
F	*Festuca ovina*	sheep's fescue
F	*Festuca pratensis*	meadow fescue
F	*Holcus lanatus*	Yorkshire fog
F	*Holcus mollis*	soft grass
F	*Molinia caerulea*	purple moor
F	*Nardus stricta*	mat grass
F	*Phleum pratense*	catstail
F	*Poa annua*	annual meadow
F	*Poa nemoralis*	woodland meadow
F	*Rhynchospora alba*	white beaked sedge

Couch Grass
Quaking Grass

The British Butterflies and Skippers: their Distribution, Habitats and Larval Foodplants

HESPERIIDAE		DISTRIBUTION
Erynnis tages	Dingy Skipper	England and Wales, mainly in the south; a few places in Scotland and Ireland
Carterocephalus palaemon	Chequered Skipper	Invernessshire, Scotland; appears to be extinct in England
Thymelicus flavus	Small Skipper	Central and Southern England and Wales, common
Thymelicus lineolus	Essex Skipper	South-east England
Thymelicus acteon	Lulworth Skipper	Dorset, Devon and Lulworth Cove, Cornwall, local
Hesperia comma	Silver-spotted Skipper	The south of England only, rare
Ochlodes venatus	Large Skipper	England and Wales and extreme south of Scotland
Pyrgus malvae	Grizzled Skipper	Southern England and Wales

HABITAT	LARVAL FOODPLANT
Any rough ground where its food plant grows, particularly calcareous soils	Bird's foot trefoil (*Lotus corniculatus*) and possibly other Leguminosae
Woodland glades and rides	Grasses, *Brachypodium sylvaticum, Molinia caerulea*
Grassland, especially tall grasses with thistles and knapweed	Many soft grasses, especially *Holcus lanatus* and *H mollis* and *Phleum pratense, Brachypodium sylvaticum*
Open grassland and woodland rides and verges	Many grasses
Cliffs by the sea	Many grasses, especially *Brachypodium pinnatum*
Chalk downland with thistles and knapweed	Grasses, especially *Festuca ovina*
Grassland, cliffs and woodland verges	*Dactylis glomerata, Brachypodium sylvaticum*
Hillsides, fields and woodland glades	*Fragaria vesca, Potentilla reptans, P sterilis, Rubus fruticosus, R idaeus*

Lesser Bird's-foot Trefoil
Lady's Slipper or
Lady's Fingers & Thumbs
(*Lotus corniculatus*)

Creeping Plume Thistle
(Cnicus arvensis)

LEFT: Small Skipper *Thymelicus flavus*
Wingspan 30mm

PAPILIONIDAE

Papilio machaon	Swallowtail	East Anglia, the Norfolk Broads

PIERIDAE

Pieris brassicae	Large White	Everywhere
Pieris rapae	Small White	Everywhere
Pieris napi	Green-veined White	Everywhere
Leptidea sinapis	Wood White	Southern England and Ireland
Anthocharis cardamines	Orange Tip	Throughout the British Isles, mainly England and Wales
Colias crocea	Clouded Yellow	Migrant – mainly southern England and southern Ireland
Gonopteryx rhamni	Brimstone	Mainly central and southern England, local in Ireland

LYCAENIDAE

Lycaena phlaeas	Small Copper	Throughout Britain
Thecla betulae	Brown Hairstreak	Southern British Isles – very local and scarce
Quercusia quercus	Purple Hairstreak	Mainly southern England and Wales

In the British Isles, mainly Fens

In the wild only, *Peucedanum palustre*, but would probably eat *Foeniculum vulgare*, *Daucus carota*, *Angelica sylvestris* and carrots in captivity

Any type

All cruciferous plants especially cabbage, also nasturtiums

Any type

All cruciferous plants especially cabbage, nasturtiums and mignonette

Lanes, damp meadows, woodland

Alliaria petiolata, *Sinapis arvensis*, *Hesperis matronalis*, *Cardamine pratensis* and other Cruciferae

Woodland rides and verges, very local

Lathyrus pratensis, *L montanus*, *Lotus Corniculatus*

Hedgerows, meadows and woodland verges

Cardamine pratensis, *Alliaria petiolata*, *Hesperis matronalis*. NB larvae are cannibals

Especially clover and lucerne fields

Trifolium species, *Medicago sativa*

Woodland and shrubland

Rhamnus catharticus, *Frangula alnus*

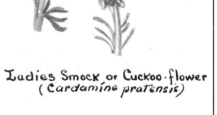

Hills and downs, open ground

Rumex acetosella, *R acetosa*

Ladies Smock or Cuckoo-flower
(*Cardamine pratensis*)

Places where there is blackthorn

Prunus spinosa

Oak woods

Quercus robur

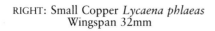

Milkwort (*Polygala vulgaris*)

RIGHT: Small Copper *Lycaena phlaeas*
Wingspan 32mm

Nordmannia w-album	White-letter Hairstreak	Central and southern England and Wales, very local, threatened by loss of elms
Nordmannia pruni	Black Hairstreak	Oxfordshire, Buckinghamshire, Huntingdonshire, Northamptonshire, rare and very local
Callophrys rubi	Green Hairstreak	Throughout British Isles especially in the south
Cupido minimus	Small Blue	Mainly southern England, uncommon, local
Celastrina argiolus	Holly Blue	England, Wales and Ireland especially in the south
Plebejus argus	Silver-studded Blue	Southern England and Wales, local
Aricia agestis	Brown Argus	Southern England and Wales
Aricia artaxerxes	Northern Brown Argus	Scotland and northern England
Polyommatus coridon	Chalkhill Blue	Southern England
Polyommatus bellargus	Adonis Blue	Southern England, local, becoming rare
Polyommatus icarus	Common Blue	Throughout the British Isles

laces where there are elms   *Ulmus glabra, U procera*

Woodland rides and verges   *Prunus spinosa*

Woodland verges and
shrubby areas

Leguminosae especially
Ulex europaeus and many
other plants

Chalk or limestone grassy
lopes and downs where
here is kidney vetch

Anthyllis vulneraria

Woodland and gardens

In spring *Ilex aquifolium*
in autumn *Hedera helix*

Heathland, downs and
oastal chalk

*Ulex europaeus, Cytisus
scoparius*, other
Leguminosae and *Calluna
vulgaris*

Downs and rough grass

*Helianthemum nummu-
larium, Erodium cicutarium*

Grassy banks and hillsides
where rock roses grow

*Helianthemum nummu-
larium*, possibly *Geranium
sanguineum*

Chalk and limestone hills
nd downs

Hippocrepis comosa

Chalk and limestone hills
nd downs

Hippocrepis comosa

ny wild grassy place,
owns

Mainly *Lotus corniculatus*,
but occasionally *Medicago
lupulina, Trifolium* species,
Ononis species, and many
other Leguminosae

Common
Gorse
or
Whin
(Ulex Europæus)

95

Common Blue *Polyommatus icarus* (ABOVE: underside)
Wingspan 35mm

Adonis Blue *Polyommatus bellargus* male
Wingspan 38mm

RIODINIDAE

Hamearis lucina	Duke of Burgundy Fritillary	Central and southern England

NYMPHALIDAE

Aglais urticae	Small Tortoiseshell	Everywhere
Nymphalis polychloros	Large Tortoiseshell	England and Wales, very rare
Inachis io	Peacock	Throughout the British Isles, especially in the south

Vanessa atalanta	Red Admiral	Everywhere, a migrant
Vanessa cardui	Painted Lady	Everywhere, a migrant
Polygonia c-album	Comma	Southern England and Wales
Argynnis paphia	Silver-washed Fritillary	South of England, Wales and Ireland
Argynnis aglaja	Dark Green Fritillary	Throughout the British Isles, especially in the south
Argynnis adippe	High Brown Fritillary	England and Wales, especially the south and west, scarce, local
Boloria selene	Small Pearl-bordered Fritillary	England, Wales and Scotland
Boloria euphrosyne	Pearl-bordered Fritillary	The British Isles

Woodland, glades, rides
and verges

Primula veris, P vulgaris

ny type

Urtica dioica

Open woodland, woodland
erges, where there are elms

Ulmus species, also *Salix,
Prunus, Populus* and
Sorbus species

ny type

Urtica dioica

Any type

Urtica dioica

Any type

Carduus and *Cirsium*
species, rarely *Urtica,
Borago, Echium*

Open woodland, hills
and gardens

*Urtica dioica, Humulus
lupulus, Ribes, Ulmus*
species

Woodland

Viola riviniana, in captivity
other *Viola* species

Open woodland, moorland,
rassland and coastal cliffs

Viola species, especially
*Viola hirta, V reichen-
bachiana, V palustris.*
Different *Viola* species are
used on different sites

Woodland verges and scrub

Viola riviniana

Woodland glades,
moorland, grassy slopes,
articularly damp places

Viola riviniana, V palustris

Woodland glades

Viola riviniana, V palustris

Marsh Violet (*Viola palustris*)

Ringlet *Aphantopus hyperantus*
Wingspan 48mm

Ringlet *Aphantopus hyperantus* (underside) on blackberry
Wingspan 48mm

Wood Spurge (*Euphorbia amygdaloides*)

Melitaea cinxia	Glanville Fritillary	Isle of Wight
Melitaea athalia	Heath Fritillary	Few localities in west and south-east of England, very rare
Euphydryas aurinia	Marsh Fritillary	Mainly western England and Wales and Ireland, very local
Apatura iris	Purple Emperor	South of England, rare
Limenitis camilla	White Admiral	South of England, range spreading

SATYRIDAE

Pararge aegeria	Speckled Wood	The British Isles, especially southern England, Wales and Ireland
Lasiommata megera	Wall Brown	Mainly the southern half of the British Isles
Aphantopus hyperantus	Ringlet	Throughout the British Isles, especially in the south

Grassy cliffs and undercliff	*Plantago lanceolata*
Woodland glades in coppiced woods	*Melampryum pratense, Plantago lanceolata*
Marshland, downs	*Succisa pratensis*
Old oak woods	*Salix caprea, S cinerea*
Large woods	*Lonicera periclymenum*
Shady woodlands and rides, verges, lanes and hedges	Coarse grasses, *Agropyron repens, Dactylis glomerata, Poa annua*
Sunny places, walls, hedges and grassy hillsides	Most coarse grasses, *Dactylis glomerata*
Woodland glades and rides and hedges	Grasses, mainly *Dactylis glomerata, Poa annua, Brachypodium sylvaticum, Deschampsia caespitosa, Agropyron repens* and *Poa pratensis*

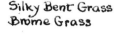

Silky Bent Grass
Brome Grass

Common Nipplewort
(Lapsana communis)

Bitter-sweet
(Solanum dulcamera)

Fine Bent Grass
(agrostis vulgaris)

Brown Argus *Aricia agestis*
Wingspan 29mm

Speckled Wood *Pararge aegeria*
Wingspan 47mm

Hipparchia semele	Grayling	The British Isles, mainly the south, and round the coast
Melanargia galathea	Marbled White	South of England
Maniola jurtina	Meadow Brown	Throughout the British Isles, especially in the south
Pyronia tithonus	Gatekeeper or Hedge Brown	Southern England, Wales, and southern Ireland
Coenonympha pamphilus	Small Heath	Throughout the British Isles, especially south of England
Coenonympha tullia	Large Heath	Scotland, Ireland, northern England, and north Wales
Erebia epiphron	Small Mountain Ringlet	Cumbria and central Scotland only, very local
Erebia aethiops	Scotch Argus	Scotland and Cumbria

rassy hillsides with bare tches of earth and rocks ar the coast	Grasses, mainly *Agropyron repens, Festuca ovina, Deschampsia caespitosa, Aria praecox*
rassland, hills and downs	Grasses, mainly *Festuca rubra, F ovina, Dactylis glomerata, Phleum pratense, Brachypodium pinnatum*
nywhere where there is ass	Grasses, especially *Poa* species
edges and lanes, oodland verges	Grasses, mainly *Festuca* species, *Dactylis glomerata. Poa annua, Agrostis tenuis*
rassland, fields, hills and wns	Small grasses, including *Poa annua, P nemoralis, Festuca pratensis*
ountainsides, moors and at bogs	*Rhynchospora alba,* possibly *Eriophorum angustifolium* and *Molinia caerulea*
mountain species. Long ass on steep slopes and mp boggy places usually ove 1500 feet	*Nardus stricta*
mountain species. stward facing slopes and oodland glades and verges here there is long grass	*Molinia caerulea, Sesleria caerulea*

Tormentil (*Potententilla tormentilla*).
Small Heath Butterfly
(*Coenonympha Pamphilus*)
Meadow Brown Butterfly.
(*Hipparchia janira*)

Adonis Blue *Polyommatus bellargus* male underside
Wingspan 38mm

HOW TO DESIGN YOUR BUTTERFLY GARDEN

Giant Campanula
(Campanula persicifolia)

Common Agrimony
(agrimonia eupatoria)

Whatever type or size of garden you may have, and whatever its location, it is possible to grow in it those plants and shrubs which will attract and support butterflies. Not only will your garden be alive with butterflies, and bees too, but it will also be attractive to look at as well as easy to manage.

A SEASIDE GARDEN

This medium-sized garden on the south coast is on the top of cliffs, and outside it there is a path leading down to the sea. In it you might get the Large, Small and Green-veined Whites, Small Tortoiseshells, Peacocks, Painted Ladies and Red Admirals, and possibly Common and Holly Blues, Meadow and Wall Browns, and Marbled Whites. Also on the cliffs would be found Small

Marbled White *Melanargia galathea*
Wingspan 58mm

Coppers, Small Heaths, Speckled Woods, Ringlets and, occasionally, Orange Tips, Commas, Brimstones and Clouded Yellows, as well as Large, Small, Grizzled and Dingy Skippers and Burnet moths. On the hills inland are localities for the Adonis Blue, the Chalkhill Blue, and the Grayling, and it is just possible that occasional vagrants of these species might visit the garden.

As you can see from the diagram the stone patio and terrace along the back of the house are raised above the garden and enclosed by a low stone wall. The patio, which could be roofed with corrugated plastic for extra protection from sea winds, provides shelter and a vantage point from which to watch the sea and the garden.

A teak seat and table, an eighteen-inch flowerpot, in the corner by the greenhouse, filled with sweet peas growing up plastic climbing plant support, and strawberry pots of Double Circus variety petunias complete the patio. Leave an unpaved space midway along the terrace by the house wall to provide a planting area for a climbing rose, such as the fragrant, bright vermilion

Grayling *Hipparchia semele*
Wingspan 56mm

A SEASIDE GARDEN

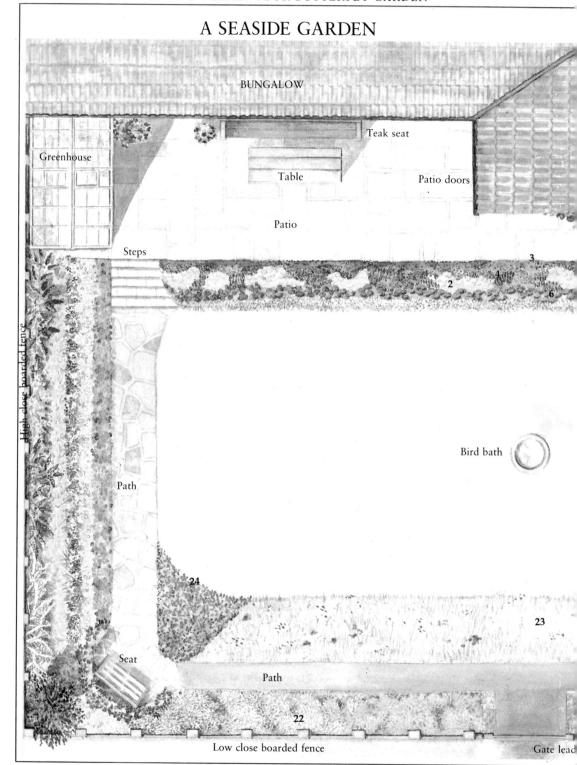

BUNGALOW

Teak seat

Greenhouse

Table

Patio doors

Patio

Steps

3

4

2

6

High close boarded fence

Bird bath

Path

24

23

Seat

Path

22

Low close boarded fence

Gate lead

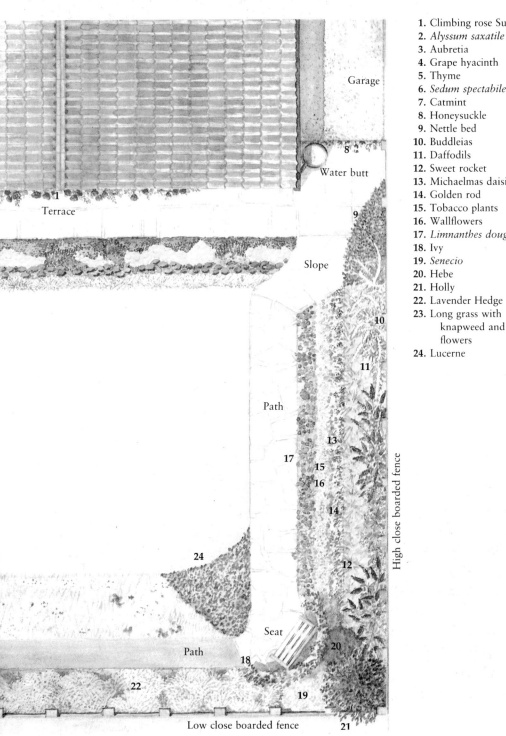

1. Climbing rose Super Star
2. *Alyssum saxatile*
3. Aubretia
4. Grape hyacinth
5. Thyme
6. *Sedum spectabile*
7. Catmint
8. Honeysuckle
9. Nettle bed
10. Buddleias
11. Daffodils
12. Sweet rocket
13. Michaelmas daisies
14. Golden rod
15. Tobacco plants
16. Wallflowers
17. *Limnanthes douglasii*
18. Ivy
19. *Senecio*
20. Hebe
21. Holly
22. Lavender Hedge
23. Long grass with knapweed and meadow flowers
24. Lucerne

Garage

Water butt

Terrace

Slope

Path

High close boarded fence

Path

Seat

Low close boarded fence

Poached egg flower *Limnanthes douglasii*

Super Star, which will require plastic climbing plant support (Netlon) on the wall. A rainwater butt stands beside the garage to catch water from the roof for watering lime-hating plants. A fine *Etrusca superba* honeysuckle grows up the garage on plastic climbing plant support.

Any building rubble left from the construction of the house, or rough stones brought from elsewhere, can be mounded along the base of the terrace wall, providing superb drainage, and then covered with at least a foot of garden soil to make a rock garden. Plant mixed shades of aubretia at the top, which will cascade down when established, and along the middle yellow *Alyssum saxatile*, grape hyacinths and thyme, while at the bottom a row of *Sedum spectabile* – the low growing pink variety, *not* Autumn Joy – and a border of catmint.

A high, close boarded fence on both sides of the garden provides protection from sea winds for a row of assorted buddleias on either side, with Golden Harvest daffodils planted between each shrub, where the bulb green can be left to die down naturally. A patch of stinging nettles is positioned near the garage. The four-foot wide border inside the buddleias is planted with a continuous row of sweet rocket at the back, then a row of alternating Michaelmas daisies and golden rod, both perennials. In front of these a row of wallflowers in the spring, and Sensation variety mixed tobacco plant in the summer, and as an edging a border of *Limnanthes douglasii*.

Orange Tip *Anthocharis cardamines* in grasses and vetch

The *Limnanthes douglasii* will flower in May and June and the plants are then left to go to seed until the end of July, when they should be taken out and shaken and the ground kept watered. In a few weeks a mass of self-sown seedlings will come up. These can be thinned out a little in September, but they should be left fairly close together, say three or four inches every way, for a mass of bloom the following year.

Inside the low close boarded fence on the sea side plant a Dwarf Munstead lavender hedge, bordering a tarred pathway. Inside this a six foot belt of long grass can be left, to be scythed only once a year in September. It can be thickly planted with knapweed (*Centaurea nigra*) and sown with packets of mixed meadow wild flowers and meadow grasses (for stockists see p 138). Plant a small patch of lucerne at either end of this belt, in memory of 1947 and other 'edusa years' of the past when this garden would have been alive with Clouded Yellows.

On either side of the holly tree in each bottom corner of the

Blossom of Holly

garden plant a *Hebe*, La Seduisante, and a *Senecio laxifolius*. In front of the holly trees is a low semi-circular stone wall with ivy growing over it, and sheltering a teak seat.

A SMALL WALLED CITY GARDEN

The yard behind this little old house measures sixteen by fourteen feet at its greatest extent and is surrounded by a six foot high brick wall. Extra space can always be created by removing any old sheds, lean-tos or coal bunkers. A lovely hawthorn tree and a great copper beech in the Cathedral Close just outside the garden wall shade the small yard in the mornings. But even in this minute space plants and shrubs essential to a butterfly garden can be grown.

The garden walls must be covered with plastic climbing plant support (Netlon) from ground level to the top of the walls. This is best done by a professional with the correct fixing attachments. All plants and climbers can then be easily tied to the Netlon for support. A fragrant, vermilion Super Star climbing rose can be trained over the kitchen door and windows, while a Swan Lake variety climbing rose planted behind the fern will spread its white weather-resistant flowers across the west wall, and a distinctive orange Schoolgirl variety climbing rose will cover part of the east wall. Choose an Early Dutch honeysuckle *Lonicera belgica* to spread between the pink Fascination buddleia in the south-west corner, and the yard door; while in the south-east corner is a holly

A SMALL
WALLED CITY GARDEN

1. Delphiniums
2. Climbing rose – Super Star
3. Mignonette
4. Sweet peas
5. Grass lawn
6. Climbing rose — Schoolgirl
7. Sweet rocket
8. *Limnanthes douglasii*
9. Copper beech tree
10. Red may tree
11. Michaelmas daisies
12. Holly
13. Tobacco plants
14. Ivy
15. Buddleia
16. Lavender
17. Honeysuckle
18. Catmint
19. Climbing rose white
    Swan Lake
20. Daffodils
21. Primroses
22. Fern
23. Aubretia

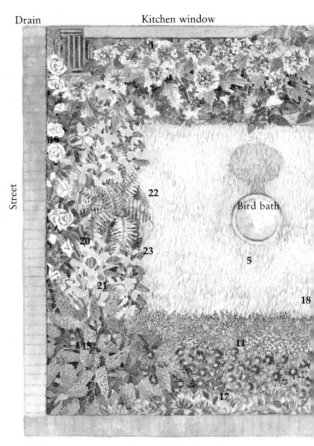

Drain Kitchen window Street Bird bath

tree and a Royal Red buddleia with ivy covering the wall behind them.

Again, sweet peas can be grown in an eighteen-inch pot, partnered by a pot of sweet-scented mignonette by the kitchen door. It might be expected that a garden of this type should be entirely paved over, but there is room for two tiny lawns, on the west four feet by five, on the east six feet by four and a half. These little lawns make all the difference to this small garden, making it a real garden rather than only a patio, and they can easily be mowed with cordless electric shears.

Under the kitchen window are pale blue Connecticut Yankee delphiniums, a short, bushy, wiry variety, and in front of them is a row of Sensation mixed tobacco plants. Around the fern plant daffodils, primroses and aubretia, with Michaelmas daisies either side of the yard door with catmint, lavender and tobacco plants. Plant a row of sweet rocket along the east wall and a border of *Limnanthes douglasii* round the east lawn.

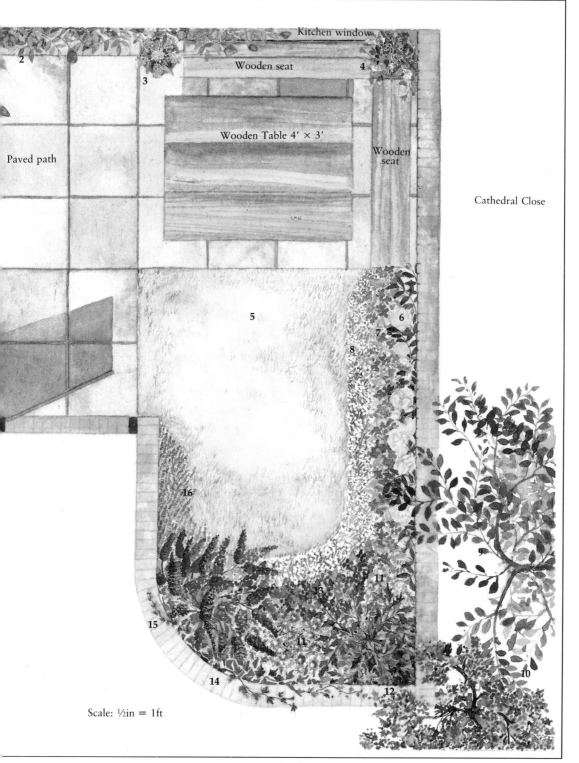

Kitchen window

Wooden seat

4

Wooden Table 4' × 3'

Paved path

Wooden
seat

2

3

Cathedral Close

5

6

7

8

16

9

11

13

11

15

14

12

10

Scale: ½in = 1ft

Large White *Pieris brassicae* on sweet rocket
Wingspan 63mm

Painted Lady *Vanessa cardui*
sunbathing on a path
Wingspan 65mm

Flower
of the Beech
(*Fagus sylvatica*)

In this garden you might hope to see Large, Small and Green-veined Whites, Small Tortoiseshells, Peacocks, Painted Ladies and Red Admirals, and possibly Holly Blues. It is also just possible that a vagrant from the species which inhabit the countryside outside the city might turn up in the garden. You can sit in the sun in this little patio and watch for butterflies and listen to the bells and chimes of the great cathedral.

A LARGE COUNTRY GARDEN

This garden, including the vegetable garden, extends to about three acres, on a sloping south facing hillside, with a stream at the bottom. Behind the house lies a wood of mixed conifers and deciduous trees with rhododendrons and azaleas. Here you would expect Large, Small and Green-veined Whites, Small Tortoise-shells, Red Admirals, Painted Ladies, Peacocks, Commas and Holly Blues. Possibly also Orange Tips, Brimstones, Small Coppers, Common Blues, Pearl-bordered, Small Pearl-bordered or Dark Green Fritillaries, Small Heaths, Speckled Woods, Meadow and Wall Browns, Large, Small and Dingy Skippers.

A hedge of Christmas trees (*Picea abies*) has been planted inside the north and south fences where the property adjoins the road, to help provide protection, and can be clipped like a privet hedge to a height of three or four feet. A hedge of wild bramble round three sides of the vegetable garden is very attractive to butterflies,

Fence

Se

5

Greenhouse

6

8

11

9   10

5

7

Drive

3   4

Garage

Path

Pass road

2

24

House   Terrace

23

Greenhouse   Patio

22

3   4   25

1

21

12

Par

13

Fence

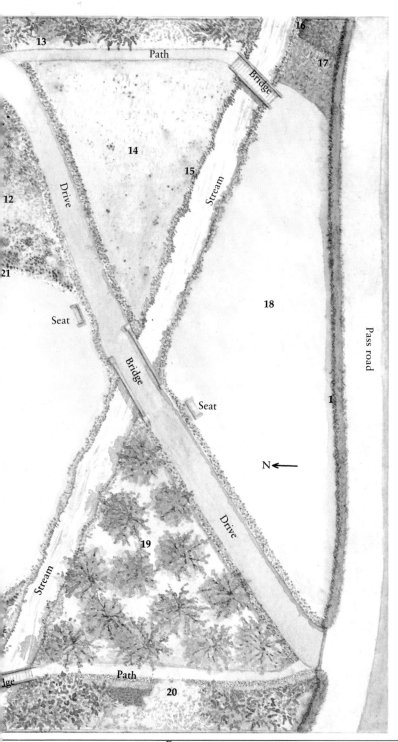

A LARGE COUNTRY GARDEN

1. Fir hedge
2. Wood
3. Willowherb
4. Daffodils
5. Brambles
6. Thistles
7. Nettles
8. Vegetable garden
9. Bramble hedge
10. Butterfly bank
11. Lavender hedge
12. Herbaceous border
13. Mixed buddleias
14. Hay meadow
15. Water mint
16. Blackthorn
17. Nettle bunker
18. Donkey field
19. Orchard
20. Bee border
21. *Limnanthes douglasii*
22. Lawn
23. Catmint
24. Climbing roses
25. Rock garden

OPPOSITE ABOVE: Climbing rose Super Star
OPPOSITE BELOW: Water mint *Mentha aquatica*
ABOVE: Rose-bay willowherb *Epilobium angustifolium*

and provides delicious blackberries in the autumn. On the side of the vegetable garden which is adjacent to the wood is a border of mixed thistles to the great delight of many butterflies. The long hedges of mixed buddleia, on the eastern and western sides, allowed to grow into one another and pruned back hard every year in April, attract all the butterflies for miles around.

Welted Thistle
(Carduus acanthoides)

Between the house and the wood hundreds of Golden Harvest daffodils have been planted in the rough grassy ground, which was then sown with rose-bay willowherb. This makes a wonderful expanse of daffodils against the background of the wood in spring, and in the summer an absolute sea of willowherb, than which there are few things more beautiful and which is a delight to many butterflies and bees. The daffodil green is allowed to die down naturally, and the only maintenance needed is scything over once a year in the autumn. Both the daffodils and the willowherb will increase year by year of their own accord.

A garden of this size provides plenty of space, so a Dwarf Munstead lavender hedge has been planted the full length of the driveway, water mint all along the stream, and a good sized nettle bunker made with a blackthorn hedge behind it. In the hay meadow near the stream, rich in wild flowers, which is scythed only once a year in early September, Blues can often be seen resting on the grass heads towards evening.

The Bee Border consists of a back row of borage, a middle row of Six Hills variety catmint and a front row of *Limnanthes douglasii*. The Butterfly Bank of rough grass is planted with clumps of viper's bugloss near the top, expanses of bird's foot trefoil and

Brimstone *Gonopteryx rhamni* feeding on a thistle
Wingspan 58mm

Wall Brown *Lasiommata megera*
Wingspan 44mm

Dark Green Fritillary *Argynnis aglaja*
Wingspan 63mm

wild thyme across the middle, and a profusion of knapweed over the lower part.

Included in the herbaceous borders, positioned according to height, with the tallest at the back, are: sunflowers, delphiniums, lupins, Michaelmas daisies, golden rod, sweet rocket, tobacco plants (Sensation), on the west; and delphiniums, sweet rocket, sweet williams, snapdragon (*Antirrhinum*), dwarf tobacco plants (Nikki) and campanulas, on the east. A continuous row of *Limnanthes douglasii* planted along the edge adjoining the lawn gives a neat finishing touch.

The buddleias at either end of the terrace beside the house are Fascination, the climbing roses growing up the terrace wall are alternately Super Star and Swan Lake. The rock garden includes *Alyssum saxatile*, aubretia, gentians, edelweiss, and small dianthus. Teak seats have been placed at various pleasant viewpoints round the garden.

THE BUTTERFLIES OF NORTH AMERICA

Eastern Tiger Swallowtail *Papilio glaucus* on garden phlox
male (BELOW) and female (ABOVE)
Wingspan 62 to 125mm

Butterfly lovers in North America are very lucky in that North America possesses far more species of butterflies than England. In America north of Mexico there are seven hundred and sixty-three species of butterflies compared with only fifty-eight in the British Isles.

It is therefore beyond the scope of this work to give a detailed list with every species as is done for the British butterflies. The following list however gives details of each subfamily. You should always try to obtain a local list for the area in which you live. A list of helpful books is given at the end of the book.

SUPERFAMILY HESPERIOIDEA – SKIPPERS

FAMILY MEGATHYMIDAE – GIANT SKIPPERS
Giant Skippers are very large Skippers, mostly called Borers in English, whose caterpillars feed on yuccas and agaves into whose leaves or stems they bore. Southern states where there are agaves or yuccas.

FAMILY HESPERIIDAE – TRUE SKIPPERS
Subfamily Hesperiinae – Branded Skippers
Branded Skippers are usually fox coloured, there are many species and their caterpillars feed on grasses. Widely distributed, especially in the south. Variety of habitats.

Subfamily Heteropterinae – Skipperlings and Arctic Skipper
Skipperlings are small dark species with small spots, found in forest glades and meadows, widely distributed. The Arctic Skipper is very distinctive, black with orange spots, and flies in damp forest glades, meadows or roadsides. Caterpillars feed on grasses.

Subfamily Pyrginae – Dusky-wings, Checquered Skippers, White, Skippers and Sooty-wings
Species of all sizes, mostly blackish, grey, dark brown, white or checquered. Caterpillars feed on a variety of plants. Widely distributed and found in many different habitats.

Subfamily Pyrrhopyginae – Araxes Skipper
The Araxes Skipper is large, dark brown with white spots and fringes. Found in the south in open woodland and roadsides. Caterpillars feed on Arizona Oak.

SUPERFAMILY PAPILIONOIDEA – BUTTERFLIES

FAMILY PAPILIONIDAE – PARNASSIANS AND SWALLOWTAILS

Subfamily Parnassiinae – Parnassians (Apollos)

Beautiful butterflies. Usually found among mountains, on rocks, in forest glades, alpine meadows and tundra. Caterpillars feed on *Sedum* and Fumariaceae and may only eat when the sun is shining on them.

Subfamily Papilioninae – Swallowtails

Large very spectacular butterflies. Wide range and wide variety of habitats. This subfamily includes the well known Anise, Black, Palamedes, Short-tailed, Spicebush and Western Tiger Swallowtails. Caterpillars eat a variety of plants particularly Umbelliferae.

FAMILY PIERIDAE – WHITES AND SULPHURS

Subfamily Pierinae – Whites

The most well known of all butterflies, some species is found almost everywhere in all different kinds of habitats. Caterpillars mainly feed on Cruciferae.

Subfamily Coliadinae – Sulphurs and Yellows

These butterflies can be yellow or orange or white. The females are often quite different from the males. They have a wide range and many different habitats. An outstanding western example is Queen Alexandra's Sulphur (*Colias alexandra*). Caterpillars usually feed on some form of Leguminosae.

Subfamily Anthocharinae – Orange Tips and Marbles

Different species occur in various parts of the continent in varying localities. Caterpillars always feed on some form of Cruciferae.

FAMILY LYCAENIDAE – GOSSAMER-WINGED BUTTERFLIES

Subfamilies Theclinae and Eumaeinae – Hairstreaks

Very attractive rather rare little butterflies, usually inhabiting woodland localities, widely distributed but often local. Caterpillars feed on trees or shrubs.

Subfamily Lycaeninae – Coppers

Eyecatching little butterflies, males bright reddish brown, some purplish – one blue – females much duller. The Blue (*Chalceria heteronea*) and the Ruddy (*Chalceria rubida*) Coppers are especial favourites. Widely distributed, mostly found in mountainous localities, some very local. Caterpillars often feed on *Rumex* species.

Monarch *Danaus plexippus* on common milkweed
Wingspan 88 to 100mm

Subfamily Polyommatinae – Blues
Very sweet little butterflies. Males are varying shades of blue, females are usually brown, undersides of both sexes pale grey or fawn with spots. Many species, widely distributed in varying habitats. Many species are common but some are rare and local. Caterpillars usually feed on some form of Leguminosae.

FAMILY RIODINIDAE – METALMARKS
Rather rare small tropical butterflies found mainly in the south and west: California, Arizona, Texas, Florida etc. Caterpillars eat a variety of plants according to the species.

FAMILY LIBYTHEIDAE – SNOUT BUTTERFLIES
The Snout butterfly is a migratory species which may be found almost anywhere in the USA, especially by streams and lakes. Sometimes mass migrations occur. The caterpillars feed on hackberries, especially *Celtis pallida*.

FAMILY APATURIDAE – LEAF-WINGS AND EMPERORS
Subfamily Charaxinae – Charaxines (Leaf-wings)
Leaf-wings are so named because the undersides resemble dead leaves. Widely distributed, especially in the south. Found in woodland verges, fields and banks of streams, very fond of rotten fruit and manure. Caterpillars feed on goatweed.

Subfamily Apaturinae – Emperors
Widely distributed. Habitat open woodland or woodland verges where there are hackberry trees. Fond of mud puddles. Caterpillars feed on trees, especially hackberry.

FAMILY NYMPHALIDAE – BRUSH-FOOTED BUTTERFLIES
Subfamily Marpesiinae – Dagger-wings
Tropical butterflies found only in the south. Caterpillars eat figs.

Subfamily Limenitidinae – Admirals and Sisters
Widespread woodland butterflies. Caterpillars feed on various trees.

Subfamily Nymphalinae – Tortoiseshells, Anglewings, Ladies and Peacocks
This subfamily includes the best known garden butterflies, the Tortoiseshells, Red Admirals, Painted Ladies, Peacocks and the Mourning Cloak. Most are widely distributed, and are found in woods, fields and roadsides as well as in gardens. Many species hibernate as adults and so are among the longest lived butterflies. Caterpillars feed on nettles, thistles, and other common weeds, some species feed on trees.

Subfamily Argynninae – Fritillaries
Brownish red butterflies with black lacy patterns. Many species, some very local, distribution widespread. One of the most familiar is the Great Spangled (*Speyeria cybele*). Variety of habitats from meadows to bogs, open woodland, to grassy mountainsides and tundra. Caterpillars of many species feed on violets.

Subfamily Melitaeinae – Checquer-spots, Patches and Crescents
A large and varied group of somewhat similar appearance to Fritillaries but the markings are less lacy. Widely distributed in very diverse habitats. Caterpillars eat many different plants.

FAMILY HELICONNIIDAE – LONG WINGS
The Zebra Longwing is a very striking, easily identified butterfly. Widely distributed, especially in the south. Habitat woods and parks, often found in gardens. Caterpillars eat passion flowers.

FAMILY DANAIDAE – MILKWEED BUTTERFLIES

The conspicuous brightly coloured (red-orange and black) Monarch or Milkweed butterfly regularly migrates in masses between the Northeast and Mexico, and congregates in great numbers on trees, especially eucalyptus and pines. The closely related species the Queen is non migratory. Distribution widespread. Habitat roadsides, fields and meadows; very fond of flowers and often seen in gardens. Caterpillars eat milkweed.

FAMILY SATYRIDAE – SATYRS AND WOOD NYMPHS

Subfamily Elymniinae –Pearly Eye and Eyed Brown
Two pretty species of woodlands and wet meadows, especially in the north. Rare and local. Caterpillars eat grasses.

Subfamily Satyrinae – Satyrs, Browns, Ringlets and Alpines
A group of fast flying tan, grey, fawn or dark brown butterflies, often rare and local, many are northern or alpine species. Habitats meadows, woodland glades, grassy mountain slopes, shale or tundra. Caterpillars eat grasses.

SOME GOLDEN RULES FOR BUTTERFLY GARDENING

1 *No* herbicides (weedkillers), insecticides, fungicides, slug, snail, worm or mole killers, or lawndressings (which usually contain weed and worm killers), or poisonous chemicals of any kind whatsoever are ever to be used.
2 The *one* thing that you can never alter is the *weather*, so *always* work in your garden if it is a fine day; never make excuses to leave it till tomorrow, for the morrow may be wet.
3 Plant everything in *masses* never in single plants.
4 Plant flowers of *one* colour rather than mixed colours.
5 Plant *single* flowers rather than double ones.
6 Plant *medium* to *pale coloured* flowers rather than dark ones.
7 Plant flowers fairly *close together*, thus leaving less room for weeds.
8 *Water* regularly.
9 *Feed* with liquid seaweed manure (Maxicrop or Sea Bounty). *Top dress* with peat, sterilized bone-meal, Acta Bacta and Forest Bark.

Creeping Cinquefoil
(*Potentilla reptans*)

USEFUL ADDRESSES

SEEDSMEN

John Chambers
(specializes in wild flowers)
15, Westleigh Road, Barton
Seagrave, Kettering, Northants
NN15 5AJ (0933 681632)

Samuel Dobie & Son Ltd
Upper Dee Mills, Llangollen,
Clwyd LL20 8SD
(0978 860119)

Suttons Seeds Ltd
Hele Road, Torquay, Devon
TQ2 7QJ (0803 62011)

Thompson & Morgan Ltd
London Road, Ipswich, Suffolk
IP2 0BA (0473 688588)

Unwins Seeds Ltd
Histon, Cambridge CB4 4LE
(0945 588522)

HORTICULTURAL NURSERIES

Cants of Colchester Ltd (Roses)
The Old Rose Gardens,
London Road, Stanway,
Colchester, Essex CO3 5UP
(0206 210176)

de Jager (Bulbs and plants)
The Nurseries, Marden,
Kent TN12 9BP (0622 831235)

Hillier Nurseries Ltd
(Plants, shrubs and trees)
Ampfield House, Ampfield,
Romsey, Hants S05 9PA
(0794 68733)

Hortico (Bulbs and plants)
Spalding, Lincs PE12 6EB
(0775 5936)

Macfarlanes Garden Centre
(Plants and shrubs)
Swingfield, Nr Dover, Kent
(030383 244)

Waterer Ltd (Shrubs)
The Nurseries, London Road,
Bagshot, Surrey (0276 72288)

Most of the above produce very
informative catalogues, with
beautiful colour illustrations,
which are sent free on request.

GARDENING EQUIPMENT

The Country Garden
PO Box 286, Langley House,
China Lane, Manchester M60 1JW
(061 2287471)

Transatlantic Plastics Ltd
Garden Estate, Ventnor,
Isle of Wight PO38 1YJ
(0983 853114)

Also Suttons Seeds, Unwins Seeds
and Samuel Dobie, see above.

BIRD FOOD

John E Haith
Park Street, Cleethorpes,
S Humberside DN35 7PQ
(0472 57515)

CLOTHES SUITABLE FOR BUTTERFLY WATCHING AND GARDENING

Damart
Bingley, W Yorks BD16 4BH
(0274 568234)

Hebden Cord Co Ltd
17–23 Oldgate, Hebden Bridge,
W Yorks HX7 6EW
(0422 843152)

CATERPILLAR BREEDING EQUIPMENT

L Christie
129, Franciscan Road, Tooting,
London SW17 8DZ (01 672 4024)

BUTTERFLY BOOKS

E W Classey Ltd
PO Box 93, Faringdon,
Oxon SN7 7DR (0367 82399)

David Dunbar
31, Llanvanor Road,
London NW2 (01 455 9612)

BUTTERFLY NEWSPAPER

Butterfly News
Lodmoor Country Park,
Weymouth, Dorset DT4 7SX
(0305 776300)

CONSERVATION OF BUTTERFLIES

The British Butterfly Conservation
Society, Tudor House, Quorn,
Loughborough, Leics LE12 8AD
(0509 412870).
The BBCS conducts Habitat
Surveys, manages Butterfly
Reserves and publishes a most
interesting magazine.
Subscription £5 pa. Why not join?

USEFUL ADDRESSES FOR US READERS

BUTTERFLY BOOKS

Flora & Fauna Books
PO 3004, Seattle,
Washington 98114 USA

Flora & Fauna Publications
4300 NW 23rd Avenue,
Suite 100, Gainesville,
Florida 32606 USA

Ward's Natural Science
Establishment Inc
11850 Florence Avenue,
Santa Fe Springs,
California 90670 USA

Wildlife Publications Inc
1014 NW 14th Avenue, Gainesville,
Florida 32601 USA

CATERPILLAR REARING EQUIPMENT

BioQuip Products
PO Box 61, Santa Monica,
California 90406 USA

Carolina Biological Supply Co
Powell Laboratories Division,
Gladstone, Oregon 97027 USA

HABITAT PROTECTION FOR BUTTERFLIES

The Xerces Society
c/o Dr Karolis Bagdonas
110 Biochemistry Building,
University of Wyoming,
Laramie, Wyoming 82071 USA

PLANTS

California Native Plant Society
Suite D, 2380 Ellsworth Street,
Berkeley, California 94704 USA

FURTHER READING

Andrews J, *The Country Diary Book of Creating a Wild Flower Garden* (Webb & Bower/Michael Joseph, 1986)

Blab J & Kudrna O, *Hilfsprogramm für Schmetterlinge* (Kilda Verlag, 1982)

Brooks M & Knight C, *The Complete Guide to British Butterflies* (Jonathan Cape, 1982)

Carter D J, *The Observer's Book of Caterpillars* (Frederick Warne, 1979)

Cribb P, *Breeding the British Butterflies* (A E S Publications, 1983)

Dealler S, *Wild Flowers for the Garden* (Batsford, 1977)

Duddington J & Johnson R, *Butterflies and Larger Moths of Lincolnshire and S Humberside* (Lincolnshire Naturalist's Union, 1983)

Feltwell J, *The Natural History of Butterflies* (Croom Helm, 1986)

Fitter R, Fitter A & Blamey M, *The Wild Flowers of Britain and Northern Europe* (Collins, 1980)

Friedrich E, *Breeding Butterflies and Moths* (Harley Books, 1986)

Garden Plants Valuable to Bees (International Bee Research Association)

Goater B, *Butterflies and Moths of Hampshire and the Isle of Wight* (E W Classey, 1974)

Goodden R, *British Butterflies* (David & Charles, 1978)

Harrison F & Sterling M J, *The Butterflies and Moths of Derbyshire* (Derbyshire Entomological Society, 1986)

Hay R & Synge P M, *The Dictionary of Garden Plants in Colour* (Ebury Press & Michael Joseph, 1975)

Heath J, *Threatened Rhopalocera in Europe* (Council of Europe, 1981)

Heath J, Pollard E & Thomas J A, *Atlas of Butterflies in Britain and Ireland* (Viking, 1984)

Higgins L G & Riley N D, *Field Guide to the Butterflies of Britain and Europe* (Collins, 1980)

Kudrna O, Ed, *The Butterflies of Europe* Vol 8, *Aspects of the Conservation of Butterflies in Europe*, (AULA Verlag, 1986)

McEwan H, *Seed Growers Guide to Herbs and Wild Flowers* (Suffolk Herbs, 1982)

Mendel H & Piotrowski S H, *The Butterflies of Suffolk, an Atlas and History* (Suffolk Naturalist's Society, 1985)

Mitchell A & Wilkinson J, *The Trees of Britain & Northern Europe* (Collins, 1982)

Newman L H, *Create a Butterfly Garden* (John Baker, 1967)

OASIS: The Magazine of Conservation Gardening Vols 1–3, 1976–80

Oates M, *Garden Plants for Butterflies* (Brian Masterton, 1985)

Reader's Digest Encyclopaedia of Garden Plants and Flowers (Reader's Digest, 1975)

Rothschild M & Farrell C, *The Butterfly Gardener* (Rainbird Press, 1983)

RSPB *Gardening with Wildlife*

Shaw J, *The Nature Photographer's Complete Guide to Professional Field Techniques* (Amphoto, 1984)

Shewell-Cooper W E, *The Complete Gardener* (Collins, 1965)

Steel C & D, *Butterflies of Berkshire, Buckinghamshire and Oxfordshire* (Pisces Publications, 1985)

Step E *Wayside & Woodland Blossoms* (Frederick Warne, 1941)

Stone J L S & Midwinter H J, *Butterfly Culture* (Blandford Press, 1975)

Thomas J, *Butterflies of the British Isles* RSNC Guide (Country Life Books, 1986)

Thomas J & Webb N, *Butterflies of Dorset* (Dorset Natural History and Archaeological Society, 1984)

Thomson G, *The Butterflies of Scotland* (Croom Helm, 1980)

Wells T, Bell S, Frost A, *Creating Attractive Grasslands Using Native Plant Species* (Nature Conservancy Council)

Whalley P, *Butterfly Watching* (Severn House, 1981)

Whalley P, *Mitchell Beazley Pocket Guide to Butterflies* (Mitchell Beazley, 1982)

Wilson R, *The Backgarden Wildlife Sanctuary Book* (Astragal Books, 1979)

ABOUT AMERICAN BUTTERFLIES

Brewer J, *Butterfly Gardening* (Xerces Society Self-help Sheet No 7, 1982)

Brown F M, Eff D, & Rotger B, *Colorado Butterflies* (Denver Museum of Natural History, 1957)

Butterfly Gardening – one way to increase urban wildlife (California edition, Xerces Society Educational Leaflet No 2, 1978)

Christensen J R, *A Field Guide to the Butterflies of the Pacific Northwest* (University Press of Idaho, 1981)

Dalton S, *Borne on the Wind: The Extraordinary World of Insects in Flight* (Reader's Digest/Dutton, New York, 1975)

Dornfeld E J, *The Butterflies of Oregon* (Timber Press, Forest Grove, Oregon, 1980)

Emmel T C & J F, *The Butterflies of Southern California* (Natural History Museum of Los Angeles, 1973)

Ferris C D & Brown F M, *Butterflies of the Rocky Mountain States* (University of Oklahoma Press, 1981)

Hodges R W & Dominick T, *Check List of the Lepidoptera of America North of Mexico* (E W Classey, 1983)

Hooper R R, *The Butterflies of Saskatchewan* (Museum of Natural History, Regina, Saskatchewan, 1973)

Howe W H, *Butterflies of North America* (Doubleday, New York, 1975)

Klots A B, *Peterson Field Guide to the Butterflies of North America East of the Great Plains* (Houghton Mifflin, Boston, 1951)

Miller L D & Brown F M, *A Catalogue/Checklist of the Butterflies of America North of Mexico* (The Lepidopterist's Society Memoir No 2, 1981)

Opler P A & Krizek G O, *Butterflies East of the Great Plains* (John Hopkins University Press, Baltimore, 1984)

Passos C F dos, *Synonymic List of Nearctic Rhopalocera* (1964)

Pyle R M, *Create a Community Butterfly Reserve* (Xerces Society Self-help Sheet No 4, 1976)

Pyle R M, *The Audubon Society Field Guide to American Butterflies* (A A Knopf, New York, 1981)

Pyle R M, *The Audubon Society Handbook for Butterfly Watchers* (Charles Scribner's & Sons, New York, 1984)

Shaw J, *The Nature Photographer's Complete Guide to Professional Field Techniques* (Amphoto, New York, 1984)

Tilden J W & Smith A C, *Peterson Field Guide to Western Butterflies* (Houghton Mifflin, Boston, 1986)

ACKNOWLEDGEMENTS

I would like to thank Dr Otakar Kudrna and Mrs Dorothy Lumley very much for their kind help and encouragement. I am also most grateful to Mrs E G Selwyn for her kind permission to use the quotation from Dean Selwyn's harvest hymn.

PICTURE CREDITS

Jeff Benn 2, 9, 18, 25, 32, 33, 34, 39 *(above, below)*, 41, 42–3, 46, 47, 56, 57, 59 *(below)*, 63, 77, 84, 88–9, 92–3, 96 *(above)*, 97, 100, 101, 105 *(above, below)*, 108, 110, 111, 127, 128, 129

Chris Burbanks 11, 21 *(above, below)*, 44 *(above, below)*, 45, 49, 64, 96 *(below)*

Biruta Akerbergs Hansen (artwork) 131, 134

Miss E J M Warren 15, 22, 26, 30, 52 *(above left, above right, below left)*, 71, 74, 75, 114, 120, 121, 124 *(above)*

Paul Wrigley (artwork) 53, 54, 58, 112–3, 118–9, 122–3

Peter Wrigley 16, 59 *(above)*, 79 *(above, below)*, 80, 81 *(above, below)*, 116, 124 *(below)*, 125

Worldwide Butterflies 17